BOB DYLAN

"Love And Theft"

AMSCO PUBLICATIONS
New York/London/Paris/Sydney/Copenhagen/Madrid

Photography by Kevin Mazur (Front cover and group)
and David Gahr (Back cover & other interior photos)

This book published 2001 by Amsco Publications,
A Division of Music Sales Corporation, New York

Order No. AM 972323
US International Standard Book Number: 0.8256.1918.1
UK International Standard Book Number: 0.7119.9134.0

EXCLUSIVE DISTRIBUTORS:
Music Sales Corporation
257 Park Avenue South, New York, NY 10010 USA
Music Sales Limited
8/9 Frith Street, London W1D 3JB England
Music Sales Pty. Limited
120 Rothschild Street, Rosebery, Sydney, NSW 2018, Australia

Printed in the United States of America by
Vicks Lithograph and Printing Corporation

Tweedle Dee & Tweedle Dum

Words and Music by Bob Dylan

1. Twee-dle-dee Dum and Twee-dle-dee Dee _____ They're
2. - 6. *See additional lyrics*

throw - ing knives____ in - to the tree_____ Two

big bags of dead man's bones____ Got their

nos - es to the grind - stones_____

E

Liv - ing in____ the Land of Nod_____

mf

repeat and fade

Additional lyrics

2. Well, they're going to the country, they're gonna retire
   They're taking a street car named Desire
   Looking in the window at the pecan pie
   Lot of things they'd like they would never buy
   Neither one gonna turn and run
   They're making a voyage to the sun
   "His Master's voice is calling me,"
   Says Tweedle-dee Dum to Tweedle-dee Dee

3. Tweedle-dee Dee and Tweedle-dee Dum
   All that and more and then some
   They walk among the stately trees
   They know the secrets of the breeze
   Tweedle-dee Dum said to Tweedle-dee Dee
   "Your presence is obnoxious to me."
   They're like babies sittin' on a woman's knee
   Tweedle-dee Dum and Tweedle-dee Dee

4. Well, the rain beating down on my window pane
   I got love for you and it's all in vain
   Brains in the pot, they're beginning to boil
   They're dripping with garlic and olive oil
   Tweedle-dee–he's on his hands and his knees
   Saying, "Throw me somethin', Mister, please."
   "What's good for you is good for me,"
   Says Tweedle-dee Dum to Tweedle-dee Dee

5. Well, they're living in a happy harmony
   Tweedle-dee Dum and Tweedle-dee Dee
   They're one day older and a dollar short
   They've got a parade permit and a police escort
   They're lying low and they're makin' hay
   They seem determined to go all the way
   They run a brick and tile company
   Tweedle-dee Dum and Tweedle-dee Dee

6. Well, a childish dream is a deathless need
   And a noble truth is a sacred dream
   My pretty baby, she's lookin' around
   She's wearin' a multi-thousand dollar gown
   Tweedle- dee Dee is a lowdown, sorry old man
   Tweedle-dee Dum, he'll stab you where you stand
   "I've had too much of your company,"
   Says Tweedle-dee Dum to Tweedle-dee Dee

Mississippi

Words and Music by Bob Dylan

Additional lyrics

2. Well, the devil's in the alley, mule's in the stall
   Say anything you wanna, I have heard it all
   I was thinkin' about the things that Rosie said
   I was dreaming I was sleeping in Rosie's bed
   Walking through the leaves, falling from the trees
   Feeling like a stranger nobody sees
   So many things that we never will undo
   I know you're sorry, I'm sorry too
   Some people will offer you their hand and some won't
   Last night I knew you, tonight I don't
   I need somethin' strong to distract my mind
   I'm gonna look at you til my eyes go blind
   Well I got here following the southern star
   I crossed that river just to be where you are
   Only one thing I did wrong
   Stayed in Mississippi a day too long

3. Well my ship's been split to splinters and it's sinking fast
   I'm drownin' in the poison, got no future, got no past
   But my heart is not weary, it's light and it's free
   I've got nothin' but affection for all those who've sailed with me
   Everybody movin' if they ain't already there
   Everybody got to move somewhere
   Stick with me baby, stick with me anyhow
   Things should start to get interesting right about now
   My clothes are wet, tight on my skin
   Not as tight as the corner that I painted myself in
   I know that fortune is waitin' to be kind
   So give me your hand and say you'll be mine
   Well, the emptiness is endless, cold as the clay
   You can always come back, but you can't come back all the way
   Only one thing I did wrong
   Stayed in Mississippi a day too long

Summer Days

Words and Music by Bob Dylan

1. Sum - mer days,
2. - 4. *See additional lyrics*

lift up your glass - es and sing_____ Ev - ery -

bod - y get read - y to lift up your glass - es and sing_____

Well, I'm stand - in' on the ta - ble, I'm pro - pos - ing a toast_ to the King_

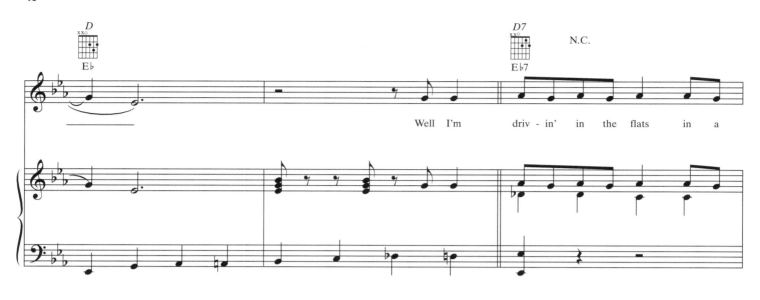

Well I'm driv-in' in the flats in a

Cad-il-lac car___ The girls all say, "You're a worn___ out star"___ My

pock-ets are load-ed and I'm___ spend-ing ev-er-y dime___

How can you say you love some-one else, you know it's me — all — the

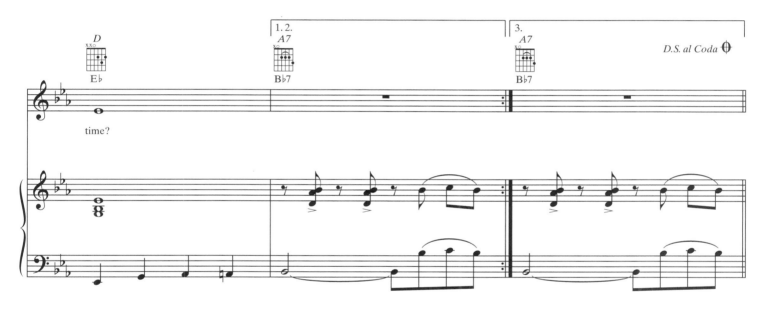

time?

I know a place — where there's still

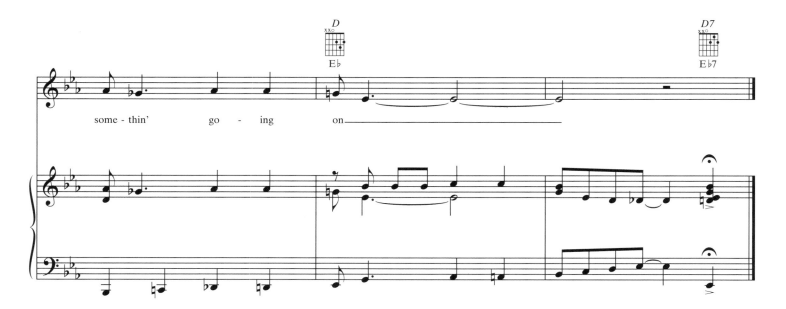

some - thin' go - ing on

Additional lyrics

2. Well, the fog's so thick you can't spy the land
   The fog is so thick you can't even spy the land
   What good are you anyway, if you can't stand up to some old business man?
   Wedding bells are ringin', the choir is beginning to sing
   Yes, the wedding bells are ringin', the choir is beginning to sing
   What looks good in the day, at night is another thing
   She's looking into my eyes, she's holding my hand
   She's looking into my eyes, she's holding my hand
   She says, "You can't repeat the past," I say, "You can't? What do you mean, you can't? Of course you can."
   Where do you come from? Where do you go?
   Sorry that's nothin' you would need to know
   Well, my back has been to the wall so long, it seems like it's stuck
   Why don't you break my heart one more time just for good luck

3. I got eight carburetors, boys I'm using 'em all
   Well, I got eight carburetors and boys I'm using 'em all
   I'm short on gas, my motor's starting to stall
   My dogs are barking, there must be someone around
   My dogs are barking, there must be someone around
   I got my hammer ringin', pretty baby, but the nails ain't goin' down
   You got something to say, speak or hold your peace
   Well, you got something to say, speak now or hold your peace
   If it's information you want you can get go it from the police
   Politician got on his jogging shoes
   He must be running for office, got no time to lose
   He been suckin' the blood out of the genius of generosity
   You been rolling your eyes–you been teasing me

4. Standing by God's river, my soul is beginnin' to shake
   Standing by God's river, my soul is beginnin' to shake
   I'm countin' on you love, to give me a break
   Well, I'm leaving in the morning just as soon as the dark clouds lift
   Yes, I'm leaving in the morning just as soon as the dark clouds lift
   Gonna break in the roof–set fire to the place as a parting gift
   Summer days, summer nights are gone
   Summer days, summer nights are gone
   I know a place where there's still somethin' going on

Lonesome Day Blues

Words and Music by Bob Dylan

Well, to-

day has been___ a sad ol' lone - some day___

2. - 12. *See additional lyrics*

Yeah, to - day has been___ a sad ol' lone - some day___

___ I'm just sit - tin' here think - ing___ With my mind___

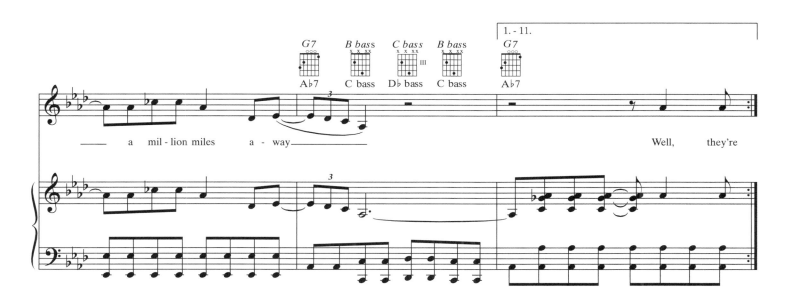

Additional lyrics

2. Well, they're doing the double shuffle,
   throwin' sand on the floor
   They're doing the double shuffle,
   they're throwin' sand on the floor
   When I left my long-time darlin'
   She was standing in the door

3. Well, my pa he died and left me, my brother
   got killed in the war
   Well, my pa he died and left me, my brother
   got killed in the war
   My sister, she ran off and got married
   Never was heard of anymore

4. Samantha Brown lived in my house for about
   four or five months
   Samantha Brown lived in my house for about
   four or five months
   Don't know how it looked to other people
   I never slept with her even once

5. Well, the road's washed out–weather not
   fit for man or beast
   Yeah, the road's washed out–weather not
   fit for man or beast
   Funny, how the things you have the hardest time
   parting with
   Are the things you need the least

6. I'm forty miles from the mill–I'm droppin'
   it into overdrive
   I'm forty miles from the mill–I'm droppin'
   it into overdrive
   Settin' my dial on the radio
   I wish my mother was still alive

7. I see your lover-man comin'–comin' 'cross the
   barren field
   I see your lover-man comin'–comin' 'cross the
   barren field
   He's not a gentlman at all–he's rotten to
   the core
   He's a coward and he steals

8. Well my captain he's decorated–he's well
   schooled and he's skilled
   My captain, he's decorated–he's well
   schooled and he's skilled
   He's not sentimental–don't bother him at all
   How many of his pals have been killed

9. Last night the wind was whisperin', I was
   trying to make out what it was
   Last night the wind was whisperin' somethin'—
   I was trying to make out what it was
   I tell myself something's comin'
   But it never does

10. I'm gonna spare the defeated–I'm gonna
    speak to the crowd
    I'm gonna spare the defeated, boys, I'm gonna
    speak to the crowd
    I am goin' to teach peace to the conquered
    I'm gonna tame the proud

11. Well the leaves are rustlin' in the wood–
    things are fallin' off of the shelf
    Leaves are rustlin' in the wood–
    things are fallin' off the shelf
    You gonna need my help, sweetheart
    You can't make love all by yourself

12. _Instrumental solo (fade)_

Bye and Bye

Words and Music by Bob Dylan

*fade on D.S. after third ending

Additional lyrics

2. Well, the future for me is already a thing of the past
   You were my first love and you will be my last
   Papa gone mad, mamma, she's feeling sad
   I'm gonna baptize you in fire so you can sin no more
   I'm gonna establish my rule through civil war
   Gonna make you see just how loyal and true a man can be

High Water
(For Charley Patton)

Words and Music by Bob Dylan

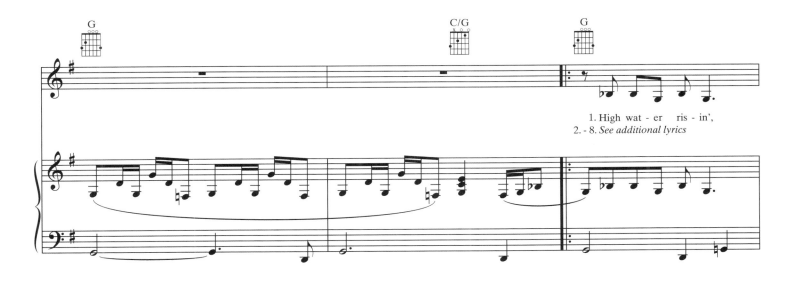

1. High wat - er ris - in',
2. - 8. *See additional lyrics*

ris - in' night and day   All the gold___ and sil - ver are be - ing stol - en a - way___ Big Joe

Tur - ner look - in' East____ and West From the dark room of his mind____ He

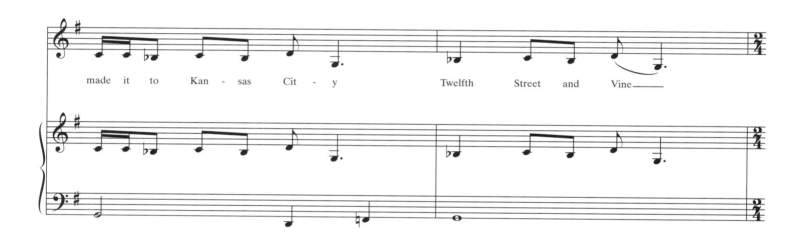

made it to Kan - sas Cit - y Twelfth Street and Vine____

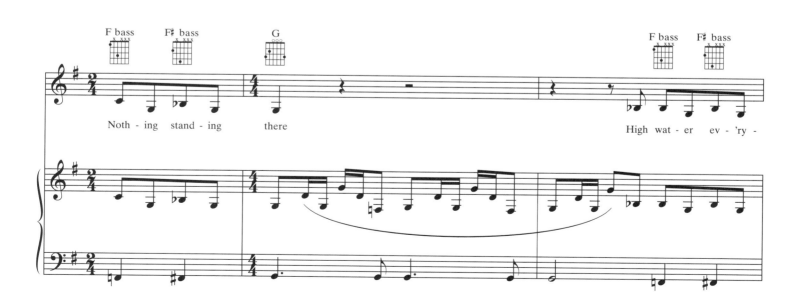

Noth - ing stand - ing there ... High wat - er ev - 'ry -

where

Additional lyrics

2. High water risin', the shacks are slidin' down
   Folks lose their possessions–folks are leaving
      town
   Bertha Mason shook it–broke it
   Then she hung it on a wall
   Says, "You're dancin' with whom they tell
      you to
   Or you don't dance at all."
   It's tough out there
   High water everywhere

3. I got a cravin' love for blazing speed
   Got a hopped up Mustang Ford
   Jump into the wagon, love, throw your panties
      on the board
   I can write you poems, make a strong man lose
      his mind
   I'm no pig without a wig
   I hope you treat me kind
   Things are breakin' up out there
   High water everywhere

4. High water risin', six inches 'bove my head
   Coffins droppin' in the street
   Like balloons made out of lead
   Water pourin' into Vicksburg, don't know what
      I'm going to do
   "Don't reach out for me," she said
   "Can't you see I'm drownin' too?"
   It's rough out there
   High water everywhere

5. Well, George Lewis told the Englishman, the
      Italian and the Jew
   "You can't open your mind, boys
   To every conceivable point of view."
   They got Charles Darwin trapped out there on
      Highway Five
   Judge says to the High Sherriff,
   "I want him dead or alive
   Either one, I don't care."
   High water everywhere

6. The Cuckoo is a pretty bird, she warbles as she
      flies
   I'm preachin' the Word of God
   I'm puttin' out your eyes
   I asked Fat Nancy for something to eat, she
      said, "Take it off the shelf–
   As great as you are a man,
   You'll never be greater than yourself."
   I told her I didn't really care
   High water everywhere

7. I'm getting up in the morning–I believe I'll
      dust my broom
   Keeping away from the women
   I'm givin' 'em lots of room
   Thunder rolling over Clarkesdale, everything
      is looking blue
   I just can't be happy, love
   Unless you're happy too
   It's bad out there
   High water everywhere

8. *Instrumental (fade)*

Floater
(Too Much to Ask)

Words and Music by Bob Dylan

Moderately, with a swing

1. Down o- ver___ the win- dow Comes the daz- zling sun- lit rays___
2. - 4. *See additional lyrics*

to Coda

___ Through the back al- leys, through the blinds___ An- oth- er

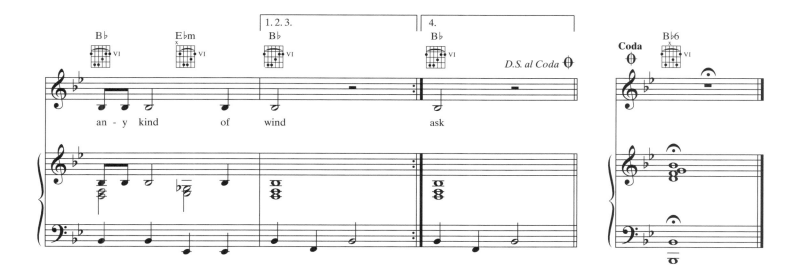

Additional lyrics

2. The old men 'round here, sometimes they get
   On bad terms with the younger men
   Old, young, age don't carry weight
   It doesn't matter in the end
   One of the boss' hangers-on
   Comes to call at times you least expect
   Try to bully ya–strong arm you–inspire you with fear
   It has the opposite effect
   There's a new grove of trees on the outskirts of town
   The old one is long gone
   Timber two-foot six across
   Burns with the bark still on
   They say, times are hard, If you don't believe it
   You can just follow your nose
   It don't bother me–times are hard everywhere
   We'll just have to see how it goes

3. My old man, he's like some feudal lord
   Got more lives than a cat
   Never seen him quarrel with my mother even once
   Things come alive or they fall flat
   You can smell the pine wood burnin'
   You can hear the school bell ring
   Gotta get up near the teacher if you can
   If you wanna learn anything
   Romeo, he said to Juliet, "You got a poor complexion.
   It doesn't give your appearance a very youthful touch!"
   Juliet said back to Romeo, "Why don't you just shove off
   If it bothers you so much."
   They all got out of here any way they could
   The cold rain can give you the shivers
   They went down the Ohio, The Cumberland, The Tennessee
   All the rest of them rebel rivers

4. If you ever try to interfere with me or cross my path again
   You do so at the peril of your own life
   I'm not quite as cool or forgiving as I sound
   I've seen enough heartaches and strife
   My grandfather was a duck trapper
   He could do it with just dragnets and ropes
   My grandmother could sew new dresses out of old cloth
   I don't know if they had any dreams or hopes
   I had 'em once though, I suppose, to go along
   With all the ring dancin' Christmas carols on all of the Christmas eves
   I left all my dreams and hopes
   Buried under tobacco leaves
   It's not always easy kicking someone out
   Gotta wait a while–it can be an unpleasant task
   Sometimes somebody wants you to give something up
   And tears or not, it's too much to ask

Moonlight

Words and Music by Bob Dylan

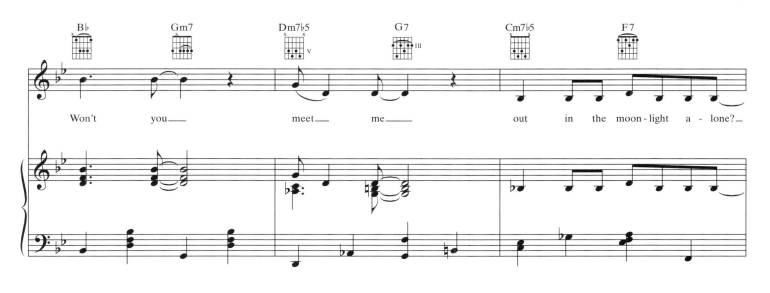

Won't you___ meet___ me___ out in the moon - light a - lone?___

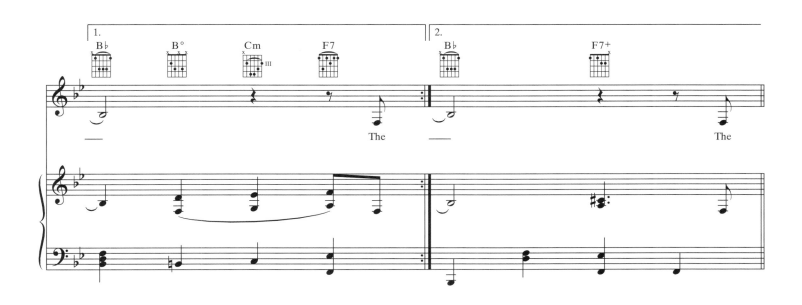

1. The 2. The

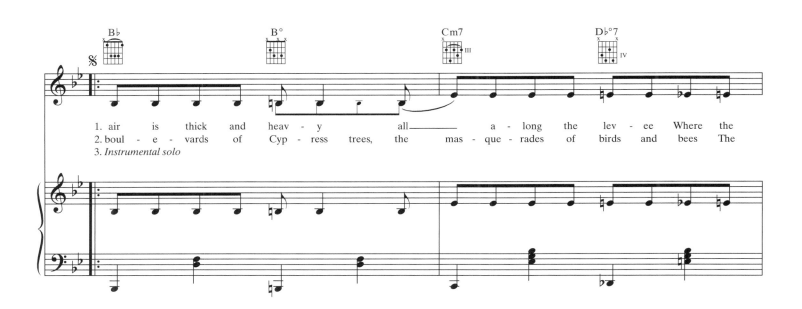

1. air is thick and heav - y all_____ a - long the lev - ee Where the
2. boul - e - vards of Cyp - ress trees, the mas - que - rades of birds and bees The
3. *Instrumental solo*

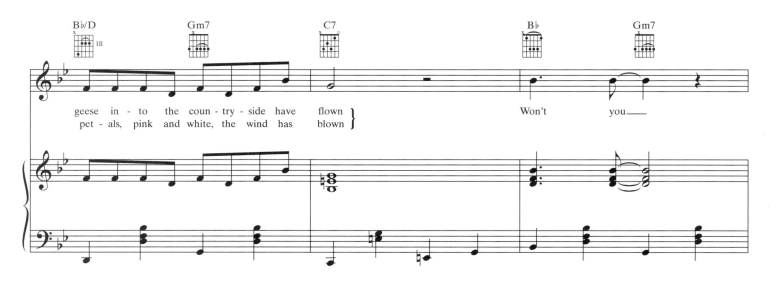

geese in-to the coun-try-side have flown }
pet-als, pink and white, the wind has blown }
Won't you___

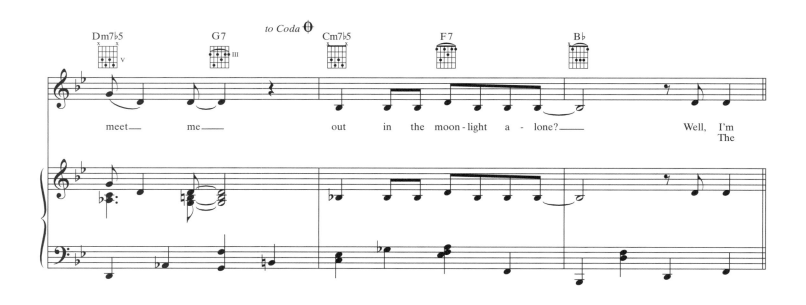

meet___ me___ out in the moon-light a - lone?___ Well, I'm
The

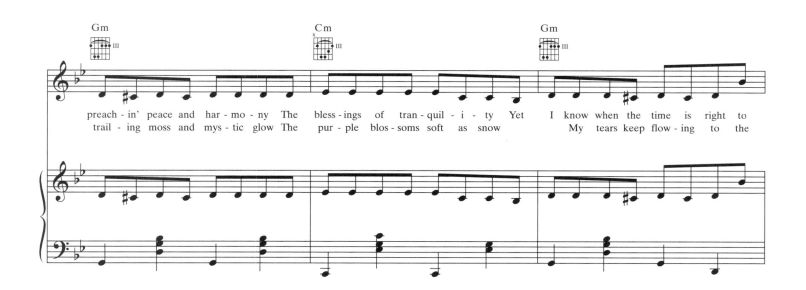

preach-in' peace and har-mo-ny The bless-ings of tran-quil-i-ty Yet I know when the time is right to
trail-ing moss and mys-tic glow The pur-ple blos-soms soft as snow My tears keep flow-ing to the

strike
sea
I'll take you 'cross the riv - er, dear You've no need to lin - ger here
Doc - tor, law - yer, In - dian chief It takes a thief to catch a thief For

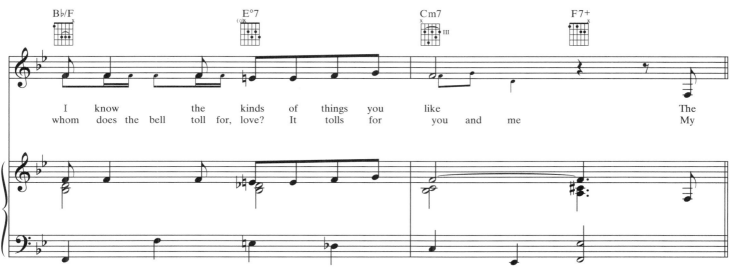

I know the kinds of things you like The
whom does the bell toll for, love? It tolls for you and me My

clouds are turn - in' crim - son, the leaves fall from the limbs an' The branch - es cast their sha - dows o - ver
pulse is run - nin' through my palm the sharp hills are ris - ing from The yel - low fields with twist - ed oaks that

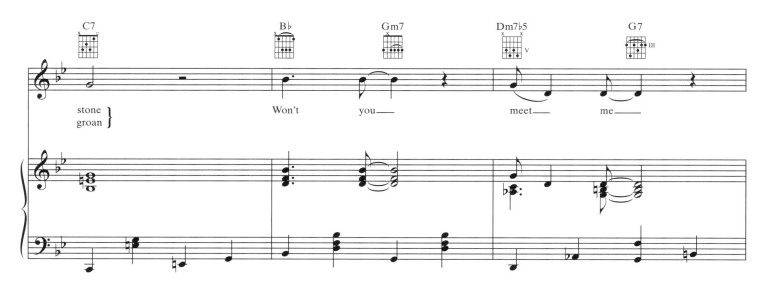

stone
groan } Won't you___ meet___ me___

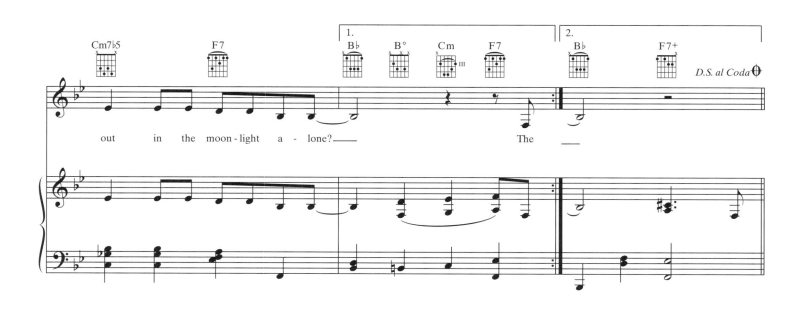

out in the moon-light a - lone?___ The ___

D.S. al Coda

Coda

N.C.

rit.   *freely (legato)*

Po' Boy

Words and Music by Bob Dylan

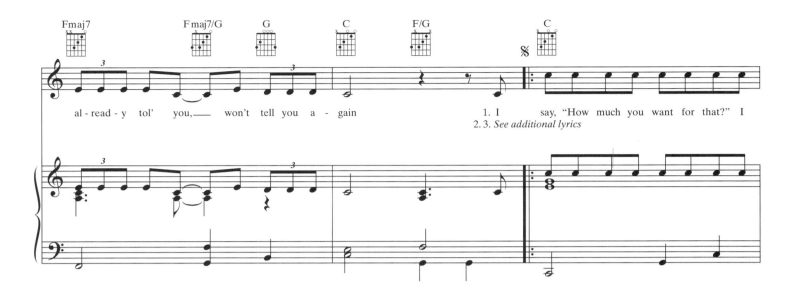

al - read - y tol' you,___ won't tell you a - gain

1. I say, "How much you want for that?" I
2. 3. *See additional lyrics*

go in - to the store___ The man says, "Three dol - lars,"___ "All right," I say, "Will you take four?"___

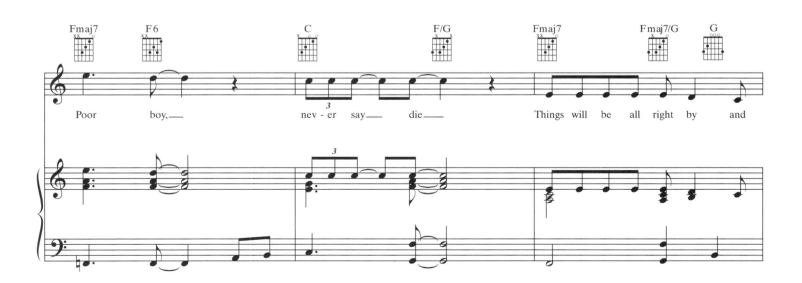

Poor boy,___ nev - er say___ die___ Things will be all right by and

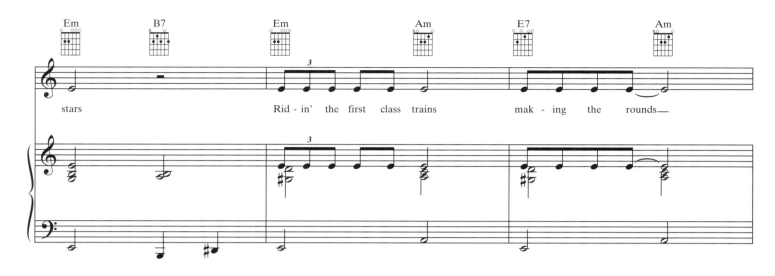

stars   Rid - in' the first class trains   mak - ing the rounds——

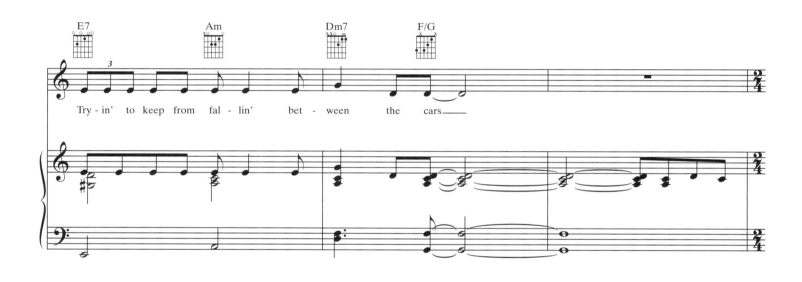

Try - in' to keep from fal - lin' bet - ween the cars——

1.   2.   *D.S. al Coda*

Oth - el - lo

Additional lyrics

2. Othello told Desdemona, "I'm cold, cover me with a blanket.
By the way, what happened to that poison wine?"
She says, "I gave it to you, you drank it."
Poor boy, layin' 'em straight–pickin' up the cherries fallin' off the plate
Time and love has branded me with its claws
Had to go to Florida, dodgin' them Georgia laws
Poor boy, in the hotel called the Palace of Gloom
Calls down to room service, says send up a room
My mother was a daughter of a wealthy farmer
My father was a traveling salesman, I never met him
When my mother died, my uncle took me in–he ran a funeral parlor
He did a lot of nice things for me and I won't forget him

3. All that I know is that I'm thrilled by your kiss
I don't know any more than this
Poor boy, pickin' up sticks
Build ya a house out of mortar and bricks
Knockin' on the door, I say, "Who is it and where are you from?"
Man says, "Freddy!" I say, "Freddy who?" He says, "Freddy or not here I come."
Poor boy 'neath the stars that shine
Washin' them dishes, feedin' them swine

Honest with Me

Words and Music by Bob Dylan

Moderately fast

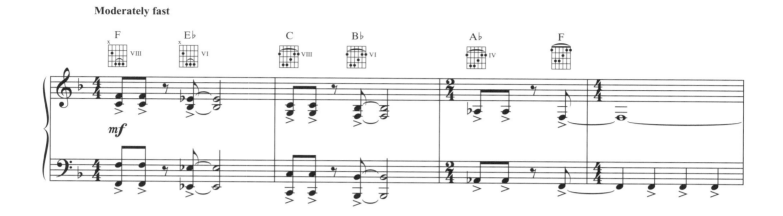

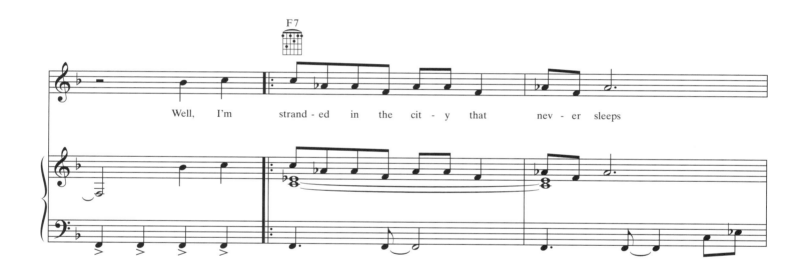

Well, I'm strand-ed in the cit-y that nev-er sleeps

Some of these wom-en they just

Additional lyrics

2. I'm not sorry for nothin' I've done
I'm glad I fought–I only wish we'd won
The Siamese twins are comin' to town
People can't wait–they're gathered around
When I left my home the sky split open wide
I never wanted to go back there–I'd rather have died
You don't understand it–my feelings for you
You'd be honest with me if only you knew

3. My woman got a face like a teddy bear
She's tossin' a baseball bat in the air
The meat is so tough you can't cut it with a sword
I'm crashin' my car, trunk first into the boards
You say my eyes are pretty and my smile is nice
Well, I'll sell it to ya at a reduced price
You don't understand it–my feelings for you
You'd be honest with me if only you knew

4. Some things are too terrible to be true
I won't come here no more if it bothers you
The Southern Pacific leaving at nine forty-five
I'm having a hard time believin' some people
were ever alive
I'm stark naked, but I don't care
I'm going off into the woods, I'm huntin' bare
You don't understand it–my feelings for you
Well, you'd be honest with me if only you knew

5. I'm here to create the new imperial empire
I'm going to do whatever circumstances require
I care so much for you–didn't think that I could
I can't tell my heart that you're no good
Well, my parents they warned me
not to waste my years
And I still got their advice oozing out of my ears
You don't understand it–my feelings for you
Well, you'd be honest with me if only you knew

6. *Instrumental (fade)*

Cry A While

Words and Music by Bob Dylan

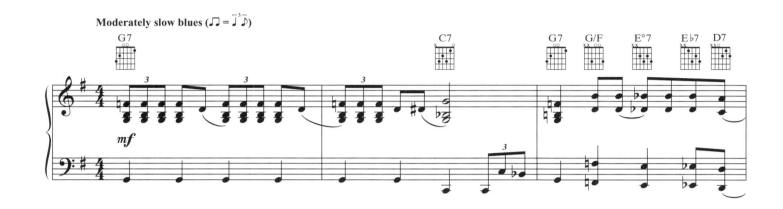

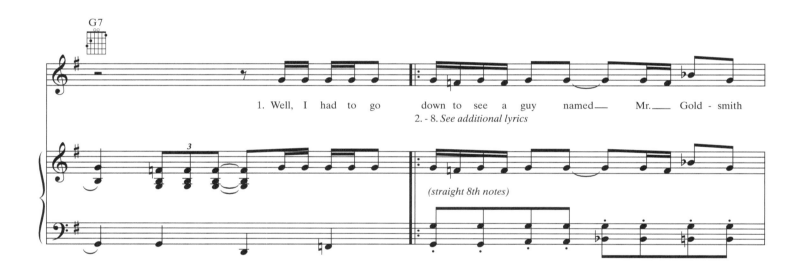

1. Well, I had to go down to see a guy named Mr. Gold-smith
2. - 8. *See additional lyrics*

(straight 8th notes)

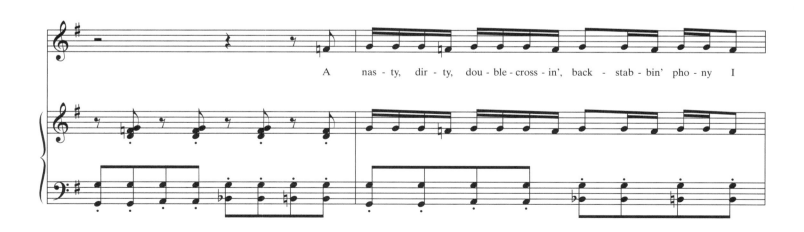

A nas-ty, dir-ty, dou-ble-cross-in', back-stab-bin' pho-ny I

did-n't wan-na have to be deal-in' with_____ But I did it for you

(swing 8th notes)

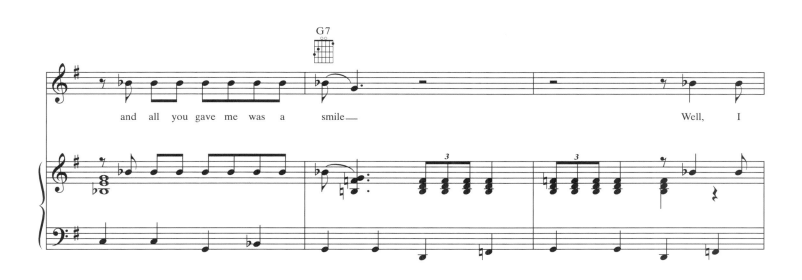

and all you gave me was a smile_____ Well, I

cried for you, now it's your turn to cry a - while_____

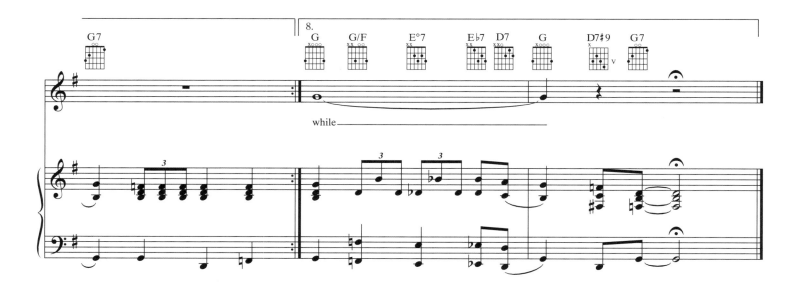

while _____

Additional lyrics

2. I don't carry dead weight—I'm no flash in the pan
   All right, I'll set you straight, can't you see I'm a union man?
   I'm lettin' the cat out of the cage, I'm keeping a low profile
   Well, I cried for you—now it's your turn to cry awhile

3. Feel like a fighting rooster—feel better than I ever felt
   But the Pennsylvania line's in an awful mess and the Denver road is about to melt
   I went to the church house, every day I go an extra mile
   Well, I cried for you—now it's your turn, you can cry awhile

4. Last night 'cross the alley there was a pounding on the walls
   It must have been Don Pasquale makin' a two A.M. booty call
   To break a trusting heart like mine was just your style
   Well, I cried for you—now it's your turn to cry awhile

5. I'm on the fringes of the night, fighting back tears that I can't control
   Some people they ain't human, they got no heart or soul
   Well, I'm crying to The Lord—I'm tryin' to be meek and mild
   Yes, I cried for you—now it's your turn, you can cry awhile

6. *Instrumental solo*

7. Well, there's preachers in the pulpits and babies in the cribs
   I'm longing for that sweet fat that sticks to your ribs
   I'm gonna buy me a barrel of whiskey—I'll die before I turn senile
   Well, I cried for you—now it's your turn, you can cry awhile

8. Well, you bet on a horse and it ran the wrong way
   I always said you'd be sorry and today could be the day
   I might need a good lawyer, could be your funeral, my trial
   Well, I cried for you—now it's your turn, you can cry awhile

Sugar Baby

Words and Music by Bob Dylan